THE ATTENTION ARCHITECT

TECHNIQUES TO BOOST PRODUCTIVITY AND BUILD BETTER HABITS

PHILIP CHARLES

PROFESSIONAL PRACTICE ACADEMY

The Attention Architect: Techniques to Boost Productivity and Build Better Habits

US English spelling is used throughout this book.

EBOOK ISBN: 978-1-925996-12-8

PRINT ISBN: 978-1-925996-13-5

Published by the Professional Practice Academy

❀ Created with Vellum

BONUS SELF-ASSESSMENT

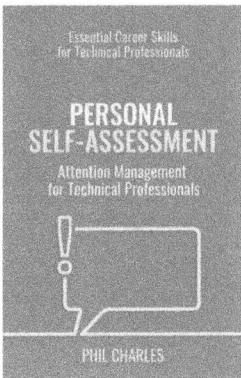

Personal Self-Assessment for *Attention Management for Technical Professionals*

The free bonus personal self-assessment quiz complements this book and is designed to help you evaluate how effectively you currently manage your attention.

To get your bonus, sign up for our email newsletter at:

https://bit.ly/attention-selfassessment

INTRODUCTION

THE POWER OF ATTENTION MANAGEMENT

Today, it is easy to feel overwhelmed by the constant stream of stimuli competing for our attention in today's information-driven society.

As technical professionals, the complexity of our tasks and the constant demand for innovation and problem-solving magnifies this challenge. To navigate these challenges effectively, attention management becomes an essential skill.

> The capacity to intentionally focus your mental energies on the tasks or activities that are most essential to you is known as **attention management**.

By mastering your attention, you can improve productivity, increase creativity, and overall satisfaction in your professional life.

There are many benefits of effective attention management. It enables you to:

1. **Enhance productivity**: You can accomplish more in less time by focusing on high-priority tasks and minimizing distractions.
2. **Boost creativity**: Improved attention management allows you to enter a state of deep focus called "flow," in which creative problem-solving and innovative thinking become more accessible.
3. **Reduce stress**: By managing your attention effectively, you can avoid feeling overwhelmed by work and maintain a healthier work-life balance.
4. **Increase job satisfaction**: When you can focus on meaningful tasks and make consistent progress, you'll experience greater accomplishment and satisfaction in your work.

In this book, you'll learn practical strategies to help you master managing your attention, specifically tailored to the needs and challenges faced by technical professionals.

WHO THIS BOOK IS FOR

This book is designed for technical professionals who want to be more successful while maintaining a healthy work-life balance. If your expertise is in science, technology, engineering, mathematics, or similar technical disciplines, then the strategies and techniques outlined in this book are highly relevant to your daily work.

Technical professionals often face unique challenges in managing their attention as their work demands focus and problem-solving abilities, and often work in dynamic environments where interruptions and distractions are common.

This book will tackle these difficulties while offering valuable tools and insights.

So, whether you are a seasoned professional or just starting your career, this book helps you take control of your attention, optimize your productivity, and thrive in your personal and professional life.

HOW TO GET THE MOST OUT OF THIS BOOK

To maximize the benefits of this book and truly master the art of attention management, it's essential to approach the content with an open mind and a commitment to applying the strategies and techniques in your daily life.

Here are some suggestions to help you get the most out of your reading experience:

1. **Read actively**: As you read, take notes, underline key points, and jot down your thoughts and reflections. Engaging with the material this way will help you retain the information and make it more applicable.
2. **Reflect on your experiences**: Throughout the book, you'll find reflection questions designed to help you evaluate your current attention management skills and identify areas for improvement. Consider these questions carefully, particularly how they apply to your personal and professional life.
3. **Apply the strategies**: This book has practical tips and techniques to improve attention management. However, reading about them is only the first step. To truly benefit from these strategies, you need to implement them in your daily life. Start by selecting one or two techniques that resonate with you and commit to practicing them consistently.
4. **Track your progress**: As you begin to apply the attention management strategies discussed in this book, make an effort to monitor your progress. Keep a journal or log to record your successes and challenges, and use this information to refine your approach and stay motivated.
5. **Share your journey**: Discussing your attention management journey with others can provide valuable support and insights. Consider sharing your experiences with colleagues, friends, or family members who may also be interested in improving their focus and productivity. You can join online forums or social media groups for attention management and personal development.

6. **Stay curious**: Attention management is a lifelong skill that can always be refined and improved. You'll discover what works best for you and your unique circumstances as you develop attention management skills. Stay open to learning new techniques, and don't be afraid to adjust your approach as needed.

By actively engaging with the material, applying the strategies, and staying committed to your attention management journey, you'll be well on your way to unlocking your full potential and achieving greater success in your personal and professional life.

~

1 UNDERSTANDING ATTENTION MANAGEMENT

1.1 DEFINING ATTENTION MANAGEMENT

Attention management is the practice of consciously directing your mental resources to focus on specific tasks or activities that align with your priorities and goals. It involves maintaining focus, filtering out distractions, and selectively engaging with stimuli in your environment. Attention management is the skill of deciding where to allocate your cognitive energy to optimize productivity, creativity, and overall well-being.

In contrast to traditional time management techniques, which focus on organizing and scheduling tasks, attention management emphasizes the quality of mental engagement during task execution. By developing strong attention management skills, you can make the most of your time and ensure that your mental energy is spent on activities that contribute to your personal and professional growth.

There are several components to effective attention management, including:

1. Prioritizing: Identifying the tasks and activities that are most important to your goals and dedicating sufficient mental resources to them.
2. Focusing: Sustaining concentration on a single task or activity for extended periods, even in the presence of potential distractions.
3. Shifting: Adjusting your attention between tasks or activities as needed while minimizing the negative impact of attention residue and multitasking.
4. Resting: Recognizing the importance of mental breaks and downtime for maintaining cognitive stamina and avoiding burnout.

By mastering these components, you can unlock the full potential of your attention and enhance your performance in both your personal and professional life.

～

KEY TAKEAWAYS

- Attention management is the practice of consciously directing your mental resources to focus on specific tasks or activities that align with your priorities and goals.
- Effective attention management involves prioritizing, focusing, shifting, and resting to optimize productivity, creativity, and well-being.
- Attention management emphasizes the quality of mental engagement during task execution rather than simply organizing and scheduling tasks.

～

REFLECTION QUESTIONS

1. How would you rate your current attention management skills? Are specific components (prioritizing, focusing, shifting, or resting) more challenging than others?
2. Can you think of a recent situation where poor attention management negatively impacted your productivity or well-being? What could you have done differently in that situation?
3. What potential benefits could you experience by improving your attention management skills? How might this impact your personal and professional life?

1.2 THE BENEFITS OF EFFECTIVE ATTENTION MANAGEMENT

Mastering attention management can lead to many benefits in your professional and personal life. By consciously directing your mental resources to the tasks and activities that matter most, you can unlock your full potential and experience greater success and satisfaction. Some of the key benefits of effective attention management include the following:

1. **Increased productivity**: You can accomplish more in less time by focusing on high-priority tasks and minimizing distractions. This enables you to progress significantly toward your goals and objectives, boosting your overall performance.
2. **Enhanced creativity**: Effective attention management can help you enter a state of deep focus, known as "flow," where you are fully immersed in the task. You're more likely to generate innovative solutions and engage in creative problem-solving in this state.
3. **Reduced stress**: When you manage your attention effectively, you can avoid feeling overwhelmed by competing demands and maintain a healthier work-life balance. This can lead to lower stress levels, increased mental resilience, and improved overall well-being.
4. **Greater job satisfaction**: Focusing on meaningful tasks and making consistent progress towards your goals can lead to greater accomplishment and satisfaction in your work. This can contribute to increased job satisfaction and motivation.
5. **Improved decision-making**: Effective attention management allows you to focus on the most relevant information and avoid cognitive overload, enhancing your ability to make informed, rational decisions in both your personal and professional life.
6. **Stronger relationships**: By practicing attention management, you can become more present and engaged in your interactions. This can lead to stronger relationships and improved communication at work and in your personal life.

~

KEY TAKEAWAYS

- Effective attention management can increase productivity, enhance creativity, reduce stress, increase job satisfaction, improve decision-making, and strengthen relationships.
- By mastering attention management, you can unlock your full potential and experience greater success and satisfaction in both your personal and professional life.

~

REFLECTION QUESTIONS

1. Which of the benefits of effective attention management resonate with you the most? Why do you find these benefits particularly important or appealing?
2. What are specific areas in your personal or professional life where improving your attention management skills might have a significant impact?
3. How might improving your attention management skills affect your relationships with others? Do you believe specific interactions or relationships would benefit from increased focus and presence?

1.3 ATTENTION VS. TIME MANAGEMENT

While attention and time management are essential skills for achieving success and maintaining a balanced life, they differ in focus and approach. Understanding the distinction between the two can help you optimize your efforts and maximize your mental and temporal resources.

Time management aims to ensure you make the best use of your available time to accomplish what you set out to do. Time management primarily revolves around organizing and allocating your time effectively to complete tasks and achieve your goals. Time management strategies often involve creating schedules, setting deadlines, breaking tasks into smaller sub-tasks, and using tools like calendars and to-do lists.

Attention management emphasizes the importance of being fully present and engaged in the task rather than simply allocating time to it. Attention management, however, focuses on the quality of your mental engagement with tasks and activities. It involves consciously directing your mental resources to prioritize and focus on the most important tasks, filter out distractions, and manage your mental energy effectively.

While both skills are important, attention management is considered a higher-order skill that complements time management. By mastering attention management, you can allocate your time effectively and ensure that you are mentally engaged and focused during the time you spend on tasks. This can lead to greater productivity, creativity, and satisfaction in your work.

∼

KEY TAKEAWAYS

- Time management involves organizing and allocating time effectively to complete tasks and achieve goals.

- Attention management focuses on the quality of your mental engagement with tasks and activities, consciously directing your mental resources to prioritize and focus on the most important tasks.
- Attention management can be considered a higher-order skill that complements time management, leading to greater productivity, creativity, and satisfaction in your work.

~

REFLECTION QUESTIONS

1. How do you currently approach time management? Do you find that your time management strategies are effective in helping you achieve your goals?
2. Can you think of situations where you allocated time effectively but struggled to maintain focus or mental engagement during the task? How might attention management have helped in these situations?
3. How do you envision incorporating attention management techniques into your existing time management strategies? What changes or adjustments might you need to make to optimize both your time and attention?

~

2 PRIORITIZING IMPORTANT TASKS

2.1 IDENTIFYING HIGH-VALUE TASKS

E ffective attention management begins with identifying the tasks that hold the highest value and contribute most significantly to your personal and professional goals. These high-value tasks are the ones that will have the greatest impact on your success and overall well-being. By recognizing and prioritizing these tasks, you can ensure that your attention is directed toward the most important aspects of your work.

To identify high-value tasks, consider the following steps:

1. **Define your goals**: Start by clearly defining your short-term and long-term goals professionally and personally. Your goals should be specific, measurable, achievable, relevant, and time-bound (SMART).
2. **Break down your goals**: Break your goals down into smaller, actionable tasks. This helps you understand the steps required to achieve your goals and makes it easier to prioritize your efforts.
3. **Evaluate task importance**: Assess each task based on its importance and relevance to your goals. Consider the potential

impact of completing the task on your overall progress and success.

4. **Consider task urgency**: In addition to importance, consider the urgency of each task. Urgent tasks require immediate attention and action, while less urgent tasks can be postponed without significant consequences.

5. **Prioritize**: Based on your assessment of importance and urgency, prioritize your tasks. High-value tasks are those that are both important and urgent or have a high impact on your goals. These tasks should receive most of your attention and focus.

6. **Re-evaluate regularly**: Your priorities may change as you progress toward your goals or as new tasks and challenges arise. Regularly re-evaluate your task priorities to ensure that your attention remains focused on the most important and relevant tasks.

By following these steps, you can clearly understand your high-value tasks and allocate your attention and mental resources accordingly. This will enable you to make the most of your time and effort, resulting in greater productivity and success in achieving your goals.

∿

KEY TAKEAWAYS

- Identifying high-value tasks is a crucial step in effective attention management.
- High-value tasks have the greatest impact on your personal and professional goals.
- Prioritize tasks based on their importance, urgency, and potential impact on your success.
- Regularly re-evaluate your task priorities to ensure that your attention remains focused on the most important and relevant tasks.

~

REFLECTION QUESTIONS

1. What are your current personal and professional goals? Are they clearly defined and specific?
2. Can you identify the high-value tasks that contribute the most to achieving your goals? Are there any tasks that consume a significant amount of your time but have little impact on your goals?
3. How often do you re-evaluate your task priorities? Are there any recent changes in your personal or professional life that may require a shift in your priorities?

2.2 THE EISENHOWER MATRIX

The Eisenhower Matrix, also known as the Urgent-Important Matrix, is a time-tested prioritization tool that can help you effectively categorize and prioritize your tasks. Developed by President Dwight D. Eisenhower, this matrix enables you to distinguish between tasks based on urgency and importance, allowing you to allocate your attention and resources more efficiently.

The Eisenhower Matrix is divided into four quadrants:

1. **Quadrant I (Important and Urgent)**: Tasks in this quadrant are both important and urgent and should be addressed immediately. These tasks are critical to achieving your goals and require your immediate attention.
2. **Quadrant II (Important but Not Urgent)**: Tasks in this quadrant are important but not urgent. These tasks contribute significantly to your long-term goals, but can be scheduled for later. Focusing on Quadrant II tasks helps you proactively work towards your goals, reducing the likelihood of tasks becoming urgent.
3. **Quadrant III (Urgent but Not Important)**: Tasks in this quadrant are urgent but not important. These tasks often involve meeting the expectations of others and can be delegated or streamlined, freeing up more time and attention for important tasks.
4. **Quadrant IV (Not Urgent and Not Important)**: Tasks in this quadrant are neither urgent nor important. These tasks typically consist of time-wasting activities or distractions and should be minimized or eliminated to maximize productivity.

To use the Eisenhower Matrix effectively:

1. List all your tasks and assign them to one of the four quadrants.
2. Focus on completing Quadrant I tasks first, as they are both important and urgent.

3. Schedule time for Quadrant II tasks as they contribute to your long-term goals.
4. Delegate or streamline Quadrant III tasks whenever possible.
5. Minimize or eliminate Quadrant IV tasks to maximize productivity.

Using the Eisenhower Matrix to prioritize your tasks, you can enhance your attention management skills and ensure your focus is directed towards the most important and impactful activities.

∼

KEY TAKEAWAYS

- The Eisenhower Matrix is a prioritization tool that helps you categorize tasks based on their urgency and importance.
- The matrix consists of four quadrants: Important and Urgent, Important but Not Urgent, Urgent but Not Important, and Not Urgent and Not Important.
- Focusing on Quadrant I and II tasks ensures that your attention is directed toward activities that contribute the most to your personal and professional goals.

∼

REFLECTION QUESTIONS

1. How does your current task prioritization system compare to the Eisenhower Matrix? Are there aspects of the matrix that could enhance your existing approach?
2. Think of a recent task you completed. In which quadrant of the Eisenhower Matrix would you place this task? Did you allocate appropriate attention to this task based on its quadrant?
3. Can you identify any tasks in Quadrant III or IV that you spend significant time on? How could you delegate, streamline,

minimize, or eliminate these tasks to focus on high-value activities better?

2.3 THE ABCDE METHOD

The ABCDE Method is another powerful prioritization technique that can help you manage your attention effectively by assigning a priority level to each task based on its importance and potential impact. This method, developed by Brian Tracy, encourages you to make conscious decisions about allocating your time and resources to achieve your goals more efficiently.

To implement the ABCDE Method, follow these steps:

1. **List your tasks**: Write all the personal and professional tasks you need to complete.
2. **Assign a letter**: Assign a letter (A, B, C, D, or E) to each task based on its importance and potential impact on your goals.
3. **A tasks** are the most important tasks that have significant consequences if not completed. These tasks should be your top priority.
4. **B tasks** are important tasks but have less severe consequences if not completed. These tasks should be completed after A tasks.
5. **C tasks** have no significant consequences but contribute to your overall productivity and well-being. Complete these tasks after A and B tasks.
6. **D tasks** can be delegated to others, freeing up your time and attention for higher-priority tasks.
7. **E tasks** can be eliminated without any negative consequences. Removing these tasks from your list helps you focus on the more important tasks.
8. **Prioritize within each category**: If you have multiple tasks in a category (e.g., several A tasks), assign a number (1, 2, 3, etc.) to each task based on its priority within the category. This creates a clear order of priority for your tasks.
9. **Take action**: Start working on your tasks in order of priority, beginning with A1, then A2, and so on. Proceed through each category, ensuring your attention is directed towards the most important and impactful tasks first.

10. **Re-evaluate regularly**: Reassess your task priorities and adjust your ABCDE assignments as needed. This ensures that your focus remains aligned with your goals and priorities as they develop.

Using the ABCDE Method to prioritize your tasks, you can manage your attention more effectively, maximize productivity, and consistently progress toward your personal and professional goals.

∼

KEY TAKEAWAYS

- The ABCDE Method is a prioritization technique that assigns a priority level to each task based on its importance and potential impact.
- 'A' tasks are the most important, while 'E' tasks can be eliminated without negative consequences.
- Prioritizing tasks using the ABCDE Method helps you manage your attention effectively and focus on the most important and impactful activities.

∼

REFLECTION QUESTIONS

1. How does the ABCDE Method compare to your current prioritization system? Are there aspects of this method that could improve your task prioritization and attention management?
2. Identify a recent task you completed and assign a letter (A, B, C, D, or E) based on the ABCDE Method. Do you believe you allocated appropriate attention to this task based on its priority level?

3. How could regularly reassessing your priorities using the
   ABCDE Method help you maintain focus on your most
   important and impactful tasks?

2.4 CASE STUDY: A TECHNICAL PROFESSIONAL'S APPROACH TO PRIORITIZATION

In this case study, we will explore the prioritization strategies used by Maya, a software engineer working for a technology company. She faces multiple projects, tight deadlines, and a constant influx of new tasks. By implementing effective prioritization techniques, she can manage her attention, maintain productivity, and succeed in her work.

Maya's Prioritization Techniques:

1. **Goal setting**: Maya defines her short-term and long-term personal and professional goals. She revisits these goals regularly and adjusts them as needed to ensure they remain relevant and achievable.
2. **Task breakdown**: For each goal, Maya breaks it down into smaller, actionable tasks. This helps her understand the steps required to achieve her goals and makes it easier to prioritize her efforts.
3. **The Eisenhower Matrix**: Maya uses the Eisenhower Matrix to categorize her tasks based on urgency and importance. This helps her allocate her time and attention to the most critical tasks, preventing them from becoming urgent crises.
4. **The ABCDE Method**: In addition to the Eisenhower Matrix, Maya employs the ABCDE Method to assign priority levels to her tasks. This method helps her allocate her attention to tasks based on their potential impact on her goals, ensuring she focuses on high-value activities.
5. **Regular re-evaluation**: Maya re-evaluates her priorities every week, adjusting her task assignments in the Eisenhower Matrix and the ABCDE Method as needed. This helps her maintain focus on the most important tasks as her goals and circumstances develop.

By using a combination of prioritization techniques and regularly reassessing her priorities, Maya can manage her attention effectively, navigate the demands of her work, and make consistent progress toward her goals.

~

KEY TAKEAWAYS

- Combining multiple prioritization techniques, such as the Eisenhower Matrix and the ABCDE Method, can help manage attention more effectively.
- Regularly re-evaluating your priorities ensures that your focus remains aligned with your goals as they develop.
- Breaking goals into smaller, actionable tasks makes prioritizing and allocating attention to high-value activities easier.

~

REFLECTION QUESTIONS

1. Which aspects of Maya's prioritization strategies are most helpful for your work? Are there techniques she uses that you could incorporate into your approach?
2. How often do you re-evaluate your priorities? Can you identify a recent situation where re-evaluating your priorities might have helped you better manage your attention?
3. How do you currently handle competing demands and multiple projects? Are there strategies Maya uses that you could apply to your work to improve your attention management and productivity?

~

3 CONTROLLING DISTRACTIONS

3.1 IDENTIFYING COMMON DISTRACTIONS

Controlling distractions is essential for effective attention management, especially for technical professionals who often require sustained focus to complete complex tasks. Before you can control distractions, you need to identify the most common sources that disrupt your focus and productivity.

Common distractions include:

1. **Digital distractions**: Emails, social media, instant messaging, and smartphone notifications can interrupt your focus and consume significant time.
2. **Environmental distractions**: Noisy workspaces, uncomfortable temperatures, or inadequate lighting can make it difficult to maintain concentration.
3. **Interruptions from colleagues**: Unscheduled meetings, impromptu conversations, or constant requests for assistance can disrupt your workflow and focus.
4. **Personal distractions**: Stress, anxiety, or personal issues can make focusing on work tasks challenging.

5. **Multitasking**: Attempting to juggle multiple tasks simultaneously often reduces focus and productivity, as your attention is divided between competing priorities.

Once you have identified your common distractions, you can take steps to minimize or eliminate their impact on your attention and productivity.

~

KEY TAKEAWAYS

- Identifying common distractions is the first step in controlling them to improve attention management.
- Common distractions include digital distractions, environmental distractions, interruptions from colleagues, personal distractions, and multitasking.
- Recognizing the sources of distraction in your work environment can help you develop strategies to minimize or eliminate their impact on your focus and productivity.

~

REFLECTION QUESTIONS

1. What are the most common distractions that you encounter in your work environment? How do these distractions impact your focus and productivity?
2. Are there any distractions that you may not have considered or recognized previously? How can you address these newfound distractions to improve your attention management?
3. How can you adjust your work environment or habits to minimize or eliminate the impact of common distractions? Are there strategies you can implement to control these distractions better?

3.2 TECHNIQUES FOR REDUCING INTERRUPTIONS

Interruptions from colleagues, whether in person or through digital channels, can significantly disrupt your focus and productivity. Implementing the following techniques can help you reduce interruptions and maintain your attention on high-priority tasks:

1. **Establish boundaries**: Communicate your need for uninterrupted focus to your colleagues. Inform them of your preferred communication channels and when you are most available for discussion.
2. **Schedule dedicated focus time**: Block off specific periods on your calendar for focused work, and inform your colleagues of these time blocks. During these periods, minimize or eliminate distractions, such as turning off email notifications and silencing your phone.
3. **Use "Do Not Disturb" signs or indicators**: Place a "Do Not Disturb" sign on your office door, or use an indicator on your digital communication tools to signal that you are unavailable for interruptions.
4. **Leverage technology**: Use tools and apps that help you manage interruptions, such as email filters, notification management tools, and website blockers.
5. **Prioritize and manage requests**: When colleagues approach you with requests or questions, assess the urgency and importance of each request. If possible, address urgent or important requests immediately, and schedule less urgent requests later.
6. **Delegate tasks when appropriate**: If a colleague's request can be handled by someone else or if you are not the best person to address it, delegate the task to the appropriate individual.

By implementing these techniques, you can reduce interruptions, maintain your focus on high-priority tasks, and improve your overall attention management.

∾

KEY TAKEAWAYS

- Reducing interruptions from colleagues is essential for maintaining focus and productivity.
- Techniques for reducing interruptions include establishing boundaries, scheduling dedicated focus time, using "Do Not Disturb" signs or indicators, leveraging technology, prioritizing and managing requests, and delegating tasks when appropriate.
- Implementing these techniques can help you maintain attention on high-priority tasks and improve attention management.

～

REFLECTION QUESTIONS

1. Which techniques for reducing interruptions do you already employ in your work environment? Are there additional strategies you could implement to minimize interruptions further?
2. How do you currently prioritize and manage requests from colleagues? Are there ways you could improve your approach to maintain your focus on high-priority tasks better?
3. Are there specific situations or types of interruptions that you find particularly challenging to manage? How could you adapt the suggested techniques to address these interruptions better and maintain focus?

3.3 CREATING AN ENVIRONMENT CONDUCIVE TO FOCUS

An environment that supports concentration and focus is crucial for effective attention management. Creating a workspace that minimizes distractions and fosters productivity can optimize your ability to complete high-priority tasks. Consider the following tips for creating an environment conducive to focus:

1. **Organize your workspace**: Keep your workspace clean and organized, with easy access to the tools and resources you need to complete your tasks. Clutter can be distracting and lead to wasted time searching for essential items.
2. **Optimize lighting and temperature**: Ensure your workspace has adequate lighting to reduce eye strain and maintain focus. Also, adjust the temperature to a comfortable level, as extreme temperatures can distract and hinder productivity.
3. **Minimize noise**: If you work in a noisy environment, consider using noise-canceling headphones or earplugs to reduce distractions. Alternatively, you can create a background noise more conducive to focus, such as white or soft instrumental music.
4. **Personalize your space**: Personalize your workspace with items that inspire and motivate you, such as photos, motivational quotes, or artwork. A space that reflects your personality and values can foster creativity and productivity.
5. **Take regular breaks**: Incorporate breaks into your work routine to help maintain focus and prevent burnout—use techniques such as the Pomodoro Technique to structure your work sessions and breaks effectively.
6. **Establish a routine**: Develop a consistent daily routine incorporating dedicated focus time, breaks, and collaboration opportunities with colleagues. A predictable routine can help you better manage your attention and maintain productivity.

By implementing these strategies, you can create an environment that supports focus, enabling you to manage your attention effectively and achieve your goals.

~

KEY TAKEAWAYS

- Creating an environment conducive to focus is essential for effective attention management.
- Fostering a focused environment includes organizing your workspace, optimizing lighting and temperature, minimizing noise, personalizing your space, taking regular breaks, and establishing a routine.
- A workspace that supports focus can help you better manage your attention and complete high-priority tasks.

~

REFLECTION QUESTIONS

1. How does your current work environment support or hinder your focus? Are there changes you can make to create a more conducive environment for focus and productivity?
2. Are there specific elements of your workspace, such as lighting, temperature, or noise, that you find particularly distracting? How can you address these distractions to improve your attention management?
3. How do you currently incorporate breaks and routines into your work schedule? Are there opportunities to optimize your routine to support focus and productivity better?

3.4 PRACTICAL EXAMPLE: HOW AN ENGINEER MINIMIZES DISTRACTIONS

In this practical example, we will examine the strategies employed by Jack, a software engineer, to minimize distractions and maintain focus in his work environment.

Jack's Distraction-Minimizing Strategies

1. **Organized workspace**: Jack keeps his desk clean and organized, with a designated place for each item. This helps him quickly locate tools and resources, reducing time wasted searching for items and minimizing distractions.
2. **Noise management**: Jack works in an open-plan office, which can be noisy. To counteract this, he uses noise-canceling headphones and listens to ambient music or white noise to maintain his focus.
3. **Digital boundaries**: Jack sets specific time blocks for checking and responding to emails and messages. He also uses tools to filter and prioritize notifications, ensuring he only receives alerts for important and urgent messages.
4. **Focused work sessions**: Jack uses the Pomodoro Technique to structure his workday. He sets dedicated periods for focused work, followed by short breaks, which help him maintain concentration and avoid burnout.
5. **Communication with colleagues**: Jack communicates his need for focus and establishes specific times when he is available for discussions or meetings. This reduces interruptions and allows him to maintain his attention on high-priority tasks.

By implementing these strategies, Jack successfully minimizes distractions in his work environment, allowing him to maintain focus, enhance productivity, and achieve his goals.

~

KEY TAKEAWAYS

- Minimizing distractions is crucial for maintaining focus and productivity in the workplace, particularly for technical professionals.
- Strategies such as organizing the workspace, managing noise, setting digital boundaries, implementing focused work sessions, and communicating with colleagues can help minimize distractions.
- Adapting and implementing these strategies can lead to improved attention management and increased productivity.

∾

REFLECTION QUESTIONS

1. Which of Jack's distraction-minimizing strategies do you find most relevant to your work environment? Are there strategies he uses that you could incorporate into your approach?
2. How do you currently manage noise distractions in your workplace? Can you adopt techniques Jack employs to improve your focus in a noisy environment?
3. How do you communicate your need for focus to your colleagues? Are there ways you could improve your communication to manage interruptions better and maintain your attention on high-priority tasks?

∾

4 BEING PRESENT

4.1 THE IMPORTANCE OF MINDFULNESS

Being present is essential to attention management, particularly for technical professionals who require sustained focus to complete complex tasks. Mindfulness, fully engaging in the present moment without judgment, can help improve your focus, reduce stress, and enhance your overall well-being.

BENEFITS OF MINDFULNESS

1. **Improved focus and concentration**: Practicing mindfulness lets you direct your attention to the task, improving focus and concentration.
2. **Reduced stress and anxiety**: Mindfulness can help you become more aware of your thoughts and feelings, enabling you to respond to stressors in a healthier manner and reducing anxiety levels.
3. **Increased self-awareness**: By becoming more aware of your thoughts, emotions, and physical sensations, mindfulness can

help you gain a better understanding of yourself and your reactions to various situations.

4. **Enhanced creativity**: Being present and fully engaged at the moment can help you access your creative potential and generate innovative ideas and solutions.
5. **Improved decision-making**: Mindfulness can lead to greater clarity and self-awareness, enabling you to make more informed, rational decisions.

Incorporating mindfulness techniques into your daily routine can improve attention management, enhance productivity, and promote a greater sense of well-being.

∾

KEY TAKEAWAYS

- Mindfulness, or fully engaging in the present moment without judgment, is essential for effective attention management.
- Benefits of mindfulness include improved focus and concentration, reduced stress and anxiety, increased self-awareness, enhanced creativity, and improved decision-making.
- Incorporating mindfulness techniques into your daily routine can help you manage your attention more effectively and improve your overall well-being.

∾

REFLECTION QUESTIONS

1. How do you currently practice mindfulness in your daily life? Could you incorporate additional mindfulness techniques to improve your focus and attention management?

2. In what situations do you find it particularly challenging to be present and fully engaged? How can mindfulness practices help you overcome these challenges and maintain your focus?
3. What benefits do you hope to gain from incorporating mindfulness techniques into your daily routine? How might these benefits contribute to improved attention management and productivity?

4.2 MINDFULNESS TECHNIQUES FOR TECHNICAL PROFESSIONALS

Incorporating mindfulness techniques into your daily routine can help you manage your attention more effectively, improving focus, productivity, and well-being. Here are several mindfulness techniques that are particularly beneficial for technical professionals:

1. **Breathing exercises**: Focusing on your breath is a simple yet powerful way to practice mindfulness. Take a few minutes throughout your day to close your eyes and concentrate on your inhalations and exhalations, allowing your thoughts to come and go without judgment.
2. **Body scan**: A body scan is a mindfulness technique that involves mentally scanning your body from head to toe, noticing any sensations or areas of tension. This practice can help you become more aware of your physical state and promote relaxation.
3. **Mindful walking**: Take a short walk during your breaks, focusing on the sensations of your body as you move. Pay attention to the feeling of your feet hitting the ground, the rhythm of your breath, and the movement of your arms and legs.
4. **Single-tasking**: Instead of multitasking, practice single-tasking by concentrating on one task at a time. Fully engage in the task, and if your mind starts to wander, gently redirect your attention back to your work.
5. **Mindful breaks**: Incorporate short, mindful breaks into your day to help reset your focus. Use these breaks to stretch, meditate, or practice deep breathing exercises, allowing yourself to recharge and refocus.
6. **Gratitude practice**: At the end of each day, reflect on the positive aspects of your work or personal life. This can help you develop a more positive mindset and improve your overall well-being.

By implementing these mindfulness techniques, technical professionals can enhance attention management, increase productivity, and foster greater well-being.

∼

KEY TAKEAWAYS

- Mindfulness techniques can help technical professionals improve attention management, increasing focus, productivity, and well-being.
- Techniques such as breathing exercises, body scans, mindful walking, single-tasking, mindful breaks, and gratitude practice can be incorporated into daily routines.
- Mindfulness can enhance focus, reduce stress, and promote a positive mindset.

∼

REFLECTION QUESTIONS

1. Which mindfulness techniques do you find most appealing or relevant to your work as a technical professional? How might these techniques improve your attention management and productivity?
2. How can you incorporate mindfulness techniques into your daily routine? Consider how you might schedule mindful breaks or integrate mindfulness practices into your habits.
3. Reflect on your current level of self-awareness and its impact on your focus and productivity. How might mindfulness help you gain greater self-awareness and improve attention management?

4.3 THE POMODORO TECHNIQUE

The Pomodoro Technique is a time-management method that encourages mindfulness and focus by breaking work into short, focused intervals called "Pomodoros," followed by brief breaks. This technique can be particularly beneficial for technical professionals who require sustained concentration to complete complex tasks.

STEPS TO IMPLEMENT THE POMODORO TECHNIQUE

1. **Choose a task**: Select a specific task you need to accomplish or a larger project to break into smaller tasks.
2. **Set a timer**: Set a timer for 25 minutes, the standard duration of a Pomodoro. During this time, focus solely on the task at hand.
3. **Work on the task**: Work until the timer goes off, minimizing distractions and maintaining focus.
4. **Take a short break**: Take a 5-minute break to recharge when the timer goes off. Use this time to stretch, grab a drink, or engage in another non-work-related activity.
5. **Repeat the process**: Continue working in 25-minute Pomodoros, followed by 5-minute breaks, until you complete the task or reach a predetermined number of Pomodoros.
6. **Take a longer break**: After completing four Pomodoros, take a longer break of 15-30 minutes to recharge further and prevent burnout.

Implementing the Pomodoro Technique can improve focus, maintain momentum on tasks, and enhance overall productivity.

∼

KEY TAKEAWAYS

- The Pomodoro Technique is a time-management method that promotes focus and productivity by breaking work into short intervals, followed by brief breaks.
- This technique can be particularly beneficial for technical professionals who require sustained concentration for complex tasks.
- The Pomodoro Technique can help improve focus, maintain task momentum, and prevent burnout.

∿

REFLECTION QUESTIONS

1. How does your current time management and focus approach compare to the Pomodoro Technique? What aspects of the Pomodoro Technique might benefit your work as a technical professional?
2. What challenges do you anticipate when implementing the Pomodoro Technique? How might you address these challenges to maintain focus and productivity?
3. How could the Pomodoro Technique help you balance productivity with self-care and well-being, particularly during demanding projects or periods of high workload?

4.4 CASE STUDY: A DATA SCIENTIST'S JOURNEY TO MINDFULNESS

In this case study, we will explore how Sarah, a data scientist, successfully incorporated mindfulness techniques into her daily routine to enhance her focus, productivity, and well-being.

Sarah's Mindfulness Journey

1. **Identifying the need for mindfulness**: Sarah realized that her work-related stress and multitasking habits negatively impacted her focus and productivity. She researched mindfulness techniques and integrated them into her daily routine to address these issues.
2. **Breathing exercises**: Sarah began practicing deep breathing exercises for a few minutes each morning and during breaks at work. This practice helped her reduce stress, increase self-awareness, and remain focused throughout the day.
3. **Single-tasking**: Sarah started focusing on one task at a time instead of multitasking. She found that this approach improved her concentration and reduced the time to complete tasks.
4. **Pomodoro Technique**: Sarah implemented the Pomodoro Technique to structure her workday. The technique's short, focused intervals allowed her to maintain her attention on complex tasks, while the regular breaks prevented burnout.
5. **Mindful walking**: Sarah incorporated mindful walking into her daily routine to improve her mindfulness further. She took short walks during breaks, focusing on her body's sensations and the environment around her.

By integrating these mindfulness techniques into her daily life, Sarah was able to enhance her focus, reduce stress, and ultimately become a more productive and effective data scientist.

〜

KEY TAKEAWAYS

- Incorporating mindfulness techniques into daily routines can help technical professionals, such as data scientists, improve their focus, productivity, and well-being.
- Techniques such as breathing exercises, single-tasking, the Pomodoro Technique, and mindful walking can effectively manage attention and reduce stress.
- Regular practice of mindfulness techniques can lead to lasting improvements in focus, productivity, and overall well-being.

~

REFLECTION QUESTIONS

1. Which of Sarah's mindfulness techniques do you find most relevant to your work as a technical professional? How might incorporating these techniques into your daily routine improve your focus, productivity, and well-being?
2. How do you currently manage work-related stress and its impact on your attention and productivity? What lessons can you learn from Sarah's journey to mindfulness?
3. Are any barriers or challenges preventing you from integrating mindfulness techniques into your daily routine? How might you address these challenges to enhance your focus and attention management?

~

5 MAXIMIZING FOCUS

5.1 UNDERSTANDING YOUR ENERGY PATTERNS

To maximize focus and productivity, it is essential to understand your energy patterns. Recognizing the times of day when you are most energized and focused can help you schedule your most important tasks during those periods.

DETERMINING YOUR ENERGY PATTERNS

1. **Track your energy levels**: For a week or two, log your energy levels throughout the day. Note any patterns or fluctuations in your energy, focus, and motivation.
2. **Identify peak times**: Analyze your log to identify the times of day when you are most energized and focused. These are your peak times, during which you should schedule high-priority tasks that require deep concentration.
3. **Adjust your schedule**: Based on your peak times, rearrange your daily schedule to accommodate your most important tasks during those periods. Reserve your lower-energy periods for less demanding tasks or administrative duties.

4. **Experiment and refine**: Monitor your energy patterns and adjust your schedule accordingly. As you become more aware of your energy patterns, you can further optimize your focus and productivity.

By understanding and leveraging your energy patterns, you can maximize your focus, complete your most important tasks more efficiently, and ultimately increase productivity.

∾

KEY TAKEAWAYS

- Understanding your energy patterns is crucial for maximizing focus and productivity.
- Tracking your energy levels and identifying your peak times can help you schedule your most important tasks during your most focused and energized periods.
- Adjusting your schedule based on your energy patterns and refining it over time can improve focus, efficiency, and productivity.

∾

REFLECTION QUESTIONS

1. Have you noticed any patterns in your energy levels throughout the day? How do these patterns impact your focus and productivity?
2. How might tracking your energy levels and identifying your peak times help you improve your attention management and task prioritization?
3. What adjustments can you make to your current schedule to better align with your unique energy patterns? How might these changes impact your focus, productivity, and overall well-being?

5.2 CREATING A FOCUS-DRIVEN SCHEDULE

A focus-driven schedule is designed to optimize your attention and productivity by aligning your tasks with your energy patterns and prioritizing your most important work. Here's how to create a focus-driven schedule:

STEPS TO CREATE A FOCUS-DRIVEN SCHEDULE

1. **Understand your energy patterns**: As discussed in the previous section, track your energy levels and identify your peak times to determine when you are most focused and energized.
2. **Prioritize your tasks**: Use techniques such as the Eisenhower Matrix or the ABCDE method to prioritize your tasks according to their importance, urgency, and level of focus required.
3. **Schedule high-priority tasks during peak times**: Allocate them to your peak times, ensuring you have the necessary focus and energy to complete them effectively.
4. **Block off time for deep work**: Schedule uninterrupted time for tasks requiring deep focus and concentration. During these blocks, minimize distractions and avoid multitasking.
5. **Incorporate breaks and mindfulness practices**: Include regular breaks in your schedule, as well as mindfulness practices such as deep breathing, meditation, or mindful walking, to recharge and maintain focus throughout the day.
6. **Adjust and refine**: Monitor your productivity and energy levels, adjusting your focus-driven schedule as needed to optimize your attention and efficiency.

By creating a focus-driven schedule, you can ensure that you allocate your attention and energy to your most important tasks and ultimately enhance your productivity.

～

KEY TAKEAWAYS

- A focus-driven schedule is designed to optimize your attention and productivity by aligning your tasks with your energy patterns and prioritizing your most important work.
- Creating a focus-driven schedule involves understanding your energy patterns, prioritizing tasks, scheduling high-priority tasks during peak times, blocking off time for deep work, incorporating breaks and mindfulness practices, and adjusting and refining the schedule as needed.
- Implementing a focus-driven schedule can lead to lasting improvements in focus, efficiency, and productivity.

~

REFLECTION QUESTIONS

1. How does your current schedule align with your energy patterns and focus? What changes could you make to create a more focus-driven schedule?
2. What challenges do you anticipate when creating and implementing a focus-driven schedule? How might you address these challenges to maintain focus and productivity?
3. How might incorporating breaks and mindfulness into your schedule enhance your focus, productivity, and overall well-being?

5.3 THE ROLE OF BREAKS IN SUSTAINING FOCUS

Taking regular breaks is essential for sustaining focus and productivity throughout the day. Breaks provide an opportunity to recharge, prevent burnout, and maintain a healthy work-life balance.

THE BENEFITS OF BREAKS

1. **Improved focus**: Short breaks help maintain focus by giving your brain a chance to recharge and reset, allowing you to return to your work refreshed and ready to concentrate.
2. **Reduced mental fatigue**: Prolonged work periods can lead to mental fatigue, decreasing productivity. Breaks help alleviate mental fatigue and keep your performance at an optimal level.
3. **Increased creativity**: Stepping away from a task can provide new perspectives and spark creative ideas, helping you find innovative solutions to problems.
4. **Preventing burnout**: Regular breaks can help reduce stress and avoid burnout, ensuring a healthy work-life balance.
5. **Enhanced well-being**: Taking breaks to exercise, socialize, or relax can improve mental and physical well-being.

INCORPORATING BREAKS INTO YOUR SCHEDULE

1. **Schedule regular breaks**: Include short breaks in your daily schedule, such as following the Pomodoro Technique or taking a break every hour or two.
2. **Vary your break activities**: Engage in various activities, such as stretching, walking, meditating, or a hobby, to keep your breaks enjoyable and refreshing.
3. **Disconnect from work**: Avoid work-related tasks or discussions during breaks, allowing your mind to disengage and recharge fully.

By understanding the role of breaks in sustaining focus and incorporating them into your schedule, you can optimize your attention, productivity, and well-being.

~

KEY TAKEAWAYS

- Regular breaks are essential for sustaining focus and productivity throughout the day.
- Breaks provide numerous benefits, including improved focus, reduced mental fatigue, increased creativity, burnout prevention, and enhanced well-being.
- Incorporating breaks into your schedule involves scheduling regular breaks, varying your break activities, and disconnecting from work during breaks.

~

REFLECTION QUESTIONS

1. How do your current break habits affect your focus and productivity? What changes could you make to incorporate more effective breaks into your schedule?
2. What types of break activities do you find most refreshing and rejuvenating? How can you include these activities in your breaks to optimize focus and productivity?
3. How can you fully disconnect from work during breaks to recharge and maintain a healthy work-life balance?

5.4 PRACTICAL EXAMPLE: HOW A NETWORK ENGINEER MAXIMIZES FOCUS

In this practical example, we'll explore how Alex, a network engineer, maximizes focus and productivity by creating a focus-driven schedule and incorporating effective breaks.

ALEX'S FOCUS-DRIVEN APPROACH

1. **Understanding energy patterns**: Alex started by monitoring his energy levels for two weeks, identifying his peak times as mid-morning and mid-afternoon. He adjusted his schedule to tackle high-priority tasks during these periods.
2. **Task prioritization**: Alex used the ABCDE method to prioritize tasks based on their importance, urgency, and required focus level. This helped him allocate his time and energy more efficiently.
3. **Scheduling deep work**: Alex reserved blocks of time for deep work, during which he turned off notifications and minimized distractions. This allowed him to concentrate on complex tasks without interruptions.
4. **Incorporating breaks**: Alex implemented the Pomodoro Technique, taking a short break after every 25-minute work interval. During longer breaks, he engaged in activities such as walking, stretching, or meditating to recharge.
5. **Creating a conducive environment**: Alex optimized his workspace by eliminating visual distractions, using noise-canceling headphones, and ensuring proper ergonomics to maintain focus and comfort.

By adopting a focus-driven approach, Alex was able to maximize his focus, improve productivity, and enhance his overall well-being.

～

KEY TAKEAWAYS

- Creating a focus-driven schedule by understanding energy patterns and prioritizing tasks can help technical professionals, such as network engineers, maximize focus and productivity.
- Scheduling blocks of time for deep work and incorporating effective breaks can further enhance focus and prevent burnout.
- Optimizing the work environment can contribute to sustained focus and increased productivity.

~

REFLECTION QUESTIONS

1. Which aspects of Alex's focus-driven approach are most relevant to your work? How might adopting similar strategies improve your focus and productivity?
2. How do your current break habits compare to Alex's approach? What changes could you make to incorporate more effective breaks into your schedule?
3. How could you optimize your work environment to support your focus and productivity better, as Alex did?

~

6 FINDING YOUR FLOW

6.1 THE SCIENCE OF FLOW STATES

F low states, or "being in the zone," occur when you become fully immersed in an activity, experiencing deep focus, enjoyment, and a sense of timelessness. This section will explore the science behind flow states and how they can enhance attention management and productivity.

CHARACTERISTICS OF FLOW STATES

Flow states are characterized by the following:

1. **Complete absorption**: When in a flow state, your attention is fully focused on the task at hand, and you lose awareness of your surroundings and the passage of time.
2. **Effortless concentration**: In a flow state, you experience a sense of effortless focus, as if the task is being performed automatically, without conscious thought.

3. **Increased performance**: Flow states are associated with heightened productivity and creativity, often leading to peak performance in your work.
4. **Intrinsic motivation**: Engaging in a task that induces a flow state can be intrinsically rewarding, leading to increased motivation and enjoyment.

CONDITIONS FOR ACHIEVING FLOW

According to psychologist Mihaly Csikszentmihalyi, who pioneered the study of flow, certain conditions must be met to achieve a flow state:

1. **Clear goals**: The task should have well-defined goals, providing direction and purpose.
2. **Immediate feedback**: Receiving feedback on your performance allows you to adjust your approach and focus on the task.
3. **Balance between challenge and skill**: The task should be challenging enough to engage your full attention but more manageable than overwhelming or discouraging.

By understanding the science behind flow states, you can create the right conditions for achieving flow in your work and ultimately enhance attention management and productivity.

∽

KEY TAKEAWAYS

- Flow states are characterized by complete absorption, effortless concentration, increased performance, and intrinsic motivation.
- Achieving flow requires clear goals, immediate feedback, and balancing challenge and skill.
- Understanding the science of flow states can help you create the right conditions for achieving flow in your work and ultimately enhance your attention management and productivity.

～

REFLECTION QUESTIONS

1. Can you recall a time when you experienced a flow state? What factors contributed to achieving this state, and how did it affect your performance and enjoyment of the task?
2. How might creating the right conditions for flow in your work improve your attention management and productivity?
3. What adjustments could you make to your work environment, tasks, or approach to better facilitate the achievement of flow states?

6.2 STRATEGIES FOR ENTERING AND SUSTAINING FLOW

To enter and sustain flow states, it is essential to adopt strategies that foster the necessary conditions for flow. This section will explore strategies that can help you achieve and maintain flow in your work.

STRATEGIES FOR ENTERING FLOW

1. **Clarify goals**: Set clear, achievable objectives for each task or project, providing a sense of direction and purpose.
2. **Choose challenging tasks**: Select tasks that are challenging enough to engage your full attention but so difficult to be overwhelming or discouraging.
3. **Eliminate distractions**: Minimize interruptions and create an environment conducive to focus, as discussed in Chapter 4.
4. **Focus on a single task**: Avoid multitasking, as it can hinder your ability to enter a flow state. Instead, concentrate on one task at a time.
5. **Develop a pre-task routine**: Establish a routine to signal the start of a focused work session, such as deep breathing exercises, meditation, or a brief visualization period.

STRATEGIES FOR SUSTAINING FLOW

1. **Monitor progress and adjust**: Regularly assess your progress and adjust as needed to maintain focus and engagement.
2. **Take breaks**: As discussed in Chapter 6, incorporate breaks to prevent mental fatigue and maintain optimal performance.
3. **Maintain a growth mindset**: Embrace challenges and view setbacks as opportunities for learning and growth rather than as reasons to give up.
4. **Celebrate small victories**: Acknowledge and reward your progress, no matter how small, to maintain motivation and a sense of achievement.

By implementing these strategies, you can increase your chances of entering and sustaining flow states, ultimately enhancing your attention management and productivity.

∽

KEY TAKEAWAYS

- Entering and sustaining flow states require strategies that foster flow conditions, such as setting clear goals, choosing challenging tasks, and eliminating distractions.
- Maintaining flow involves monitoring progress, taking breaks, maintaining a growth mindset, and celebrating small victories.
- Implementing these strategies can help you achieve and maintain flow in your work, ultimately enhancing your attention management and productivity.

∽

REFLECTION QUESTIONS

1. Which strategies for entering and sustaining flow resonate with you the most? How can you incorporate these strategies into your work routine?
2. How do your current work habits support or hinder your ability to achieve flow states? What changes could you make to facilitate flow in your work better?
3. Are any specific tasks or projects in your work that would benefit from applying these strategies to enter and sustain flow? How might achieving flow in these tasks impact your overall productivity and job satisfaction?

6.3 RECOGNIZING AND OVERCOMING FLOW BLOCKERS

Flow blockers can prevent you from entering or sustaining a flow state. This section will identify common flow blockers and provide strategies for overcoming them.

COMMON FLOW BLOCKERS

1. **Multitasking**: Attempting to handle multiple tasks simultaneously can hinder your ability to focus deeply and enter a flow state.
2. **Distractions**: External interruptions, such as phone notifications or noisy environments, can disrupt concentration and prevent flow.
3. **Procrastination**: Delaying tasks can create a cycle of avoidance and anxiety, making it difficult to achieve flow.
4. **Perfectionism**: Striving for perfection can result in excessive self-criticism and constant reevaluation of your work, impeding flow.
5. **Lack of motivation**: Insufficient motivation or interest in a task can make engaging fully and entering a flow state challenging.

STRATEGIES FOR OVERCOMING FLOW BLOCKERS

1. **Single-task focus**: Prioritize one task at a time and avoid multitasking to help maintain deep focus and achieve flow.
2. **Create a distraction-free environment**: As discussed in Chapter 4, minimize interruptions to maintain concentration and support flow states.
3. **Develop a pre-task routine**: Establish a routine to signal the start of a focused work session, as mentioned in the previous section, to combat procrastination.
4. **Embrace progress over perfection**: Focus on making progress rather than achieving perfection. Remind yourself that it's okay

to make mistakes and that you can always revise and improve later.

5. **Find intrinsic motivation**: Identify aspects of the task that genuinely interest or excite you. Reframe the task to emphasize these aspects and increase your motivation if possible.

Recognizing and overcoming flow blockers can enhance your ability to enter and sustain flow states, ultimately improving attention management and productivity.

~

KEY TAKEAWAYS

- Flow blockers, such as multitasking, distractions, procrastination, perfectionism, and lack of motivation, can prevent you from entering or sustaining a flow state.
- Strategies for overcoming flow blockers include single-task focus, creating a distraction-free environment, developing a pre-task routine, embracing progress over perfection, and finding intrinsic motivation.
- Recognizing and overcoming flow blockers can help you achieve and maintain flow in your work, ultimately enhancing your attention management and productivity.

~

REFLECTION QUESTIONS

1. Which flow blockers do you most frequently encounter in your work? What specific strategies can you implement to overcome these blockers and achieve flow more often?
2. How might your current work habits contribute to the presence of flow blockers? What changes can you make to minimize these blockers and facilitate flow states?

3. Reflect on a recent task or project where you faced flow blockers. How might overcoming these blockers have affected your productivity, job satisfaction, and overall performance?

6.4 CASE STUDY: A DEVELOPER'S EXPERIENCE WITH FLOW

In this case study, we'll explore the experience of Jane, a software developer, and her journey to achieving flow states in her work.

JANE'S BACKGROUND

Jane has been working as a software developer for five years. She loves coding and finds satisfaction in solving complex problems. However, she often needs help maintaining focus due to frequent interruptions and an overwhelming workload.

ENTERING AND SUSTAINING FLOW

Jane began implementing strategies to achieve and maintain flow states to improve attention management. Here's what she did:

1. **Set clear goals**: Jane started each work session by setting specific, achievable objectives for the tasks she needed to complete.
2. **Eliminate distractions**: She turned off her phone notifications and used noise-canceling headphones to block office noise.
3. **Develop a pre-task routine**: Jane began her work sessions with a short breathing exercise to signal her brain that it was time to focus.
4. **Monitor progress and adjust**: She assessed her progress regularly and changed her approach to maintaining her flow state.

As a result of these strategies, Jane began experiencing more frequent flow states, leading to increased productivity and job satisfaction.

OVERCOMING FLOW BLOCKERS

Jane also recognized several flow blockers that were hindering her ability to achieve and sustain flow:

1. **Multitasking**: She realized that multitasking prevented her from entering a flow state, so she began focusing on one task at a time.
2. **Procrastination**: Jane identified her tendency to procrastinate and started using her pre-task routine to overcome it.

By addressing these flow blockers, Jane enhanced her ability to achieve flow and improve her attention management.

∿

KEY TAKEAWAYS

- Jane, a software developer, needed help maintaining focus and achieving flow states in her work.
- By implementing strategies such as setting clear goals, eliminating distractions, and developing a pre-task routine, Jane could achieve and maintain flow more frequently.
- Jane also recognized and overcame flow blockers, such as multitasking and procrastination, increasing productivity and job satisfaction.

∿

REFLECTION QUESTIONS

1. Can you relate to Jane's experience in struggling to achieve flow states? Which aspects of her story resonate with your work situation?

2. Which strategies Jane implemented to achieve and maintain flow could benefit you in your work routine?

3. Are there any flow blockers that you and Jane share? How can you apply Jane's strategies to your work environment to overcome these blockers?

～

7 BRINGING IT ALL TOGETHER: AN ACTION PLAN FOR ATTENTION MANAGEMENT

7.1 ASSESSING YOUR CURRENT ATTENTION MANAGEMENT SKILLS

Before creating an action plan for improving your attention management, it is essential to assess your current skills and identify areas for growth. This section will guide you through evaluating your attention management abilities and recognizing areas requiring improvement.

SELF-ASSESSMENT

To assess your current attention management skills, consider the following aspects:

1. **Prioritization**: Can you identify high-value tasks and allocate your time and energy accordingly?
2. **Distraction control**: Do you have effective strategies to minimize interruptions and maintain focus?

3. **Mindfulness**: Can you stay present and fully engaged in your work, avoiding the pitfalls of multitasking and constant task-switching?
4. **Focus and flow**: Do you regularly achieve flow states in your work, maximizing your focus and productivity?

Take some time to reflect on these aspects and honestly evaluate your current attention management skills.

IDENTIFYING AREAS FOR IMPROVEMENT

Based on your self-assessment, identify the areas where you feel there is the most room for growth. Recognizing these areas will help you create a targeted action plan to enhance your attention management skills.

~

KEY TAKEAWAYS

- Assessing your current attention management skills is an essential first step in creating an action plan for improvement.
- Consider prioritization, distraction control, mindfulness, focus, and flow when evaluating your skills.
- Identifying areas for improvement allows you to create a targeted action plan to enhance your attention management skills.

~

REFLECTION QUESTIONS

1. Which aspects of attention management do you feel are your strengths? How can you build on these strengths to further improve your attention management skills?

2. Which attention management areas do you feel you need the most improvement in? What specific strategies from the previous chapters can you implement to address these areas?
3. How can regularly assessing your attention management skills help you stay accountable and ensure continued growth in your professional life?

7.2 IMPLEMENTING YOUR PERSONALIZED ATTENTION MANAGEMENT STRATEGY

Once you've assessed your current attention management skills and identified areas for improvement, it's time to create and implement a personalized strategy. This section will guide you through developing an action plan tailored to your needs.

CREATING YOUR ACTION PLAN

1. **Set specific goals**: Define clear, measurable goals related to the areas of improvement you've identified. For example, if you need to improve your prioritization skills, set a goal to consistently apply the Eisenhower Matrix or the ABCDE Method to your tasks.
2. **Choose relevant strategies**: Select strategies from the previous chapters that align with your goals and resonate with you. For example, if you're working on controlling distractions, implement techniques for reducing interruptions and creating a focus-driven environment.
3. **Establish a timeline**: Create a timeline for implementing your chosen strategies, with milestones for tracking your progress. This will help you stay on track and maintain momentum toward your goals.
4. **Monitor progress and adjust**: Regularly assess your progress, and be prepared to adjust your action plan as needed. This may involve tweaking your strategies, setting new goals, or addressing additional areas for improvement.

IMPLEMENTING YOUR STRATEGY

1. **Commit to change**: Embrace the change process and be prepared to put in the effort required to improve your attention management skills.

2. **Stay accountable**: Share your goals and progress with a trusted colleague, mentor, or friend who can help you stay accountable.
3. **Celebrate successes**: Recognize and celebrate your achievements, both big and small, as you work toward your attention management goals.
4. **Maintain a growth mindset**: Understand that attention management is an ongoing journey, and be open to learning, adapting, and growing throughout the process.

～

KEY TAKEAWAYS

- Creating a personalized attention management strategy involves setting specific goals, choosing relevant strategies, establishing a timeline, and monitoring progress and adjustments.
- Implementing your strategy requires a commitment to change, accountability, celebrating successes, and maintaining a growth mindset.
- A tailored action plan can help you improve your attention management skills and boost productivity, creativity, and overall job satisfaction.

～

REFLECTION QUESTIONS

1. What specific goals can you set for improving your attention management skills based on your self-assessment and identified areas for improvement?
2. How can you ensure your chosen strategies and action plan are tailored to your unique needs and work environment?
3. How will you hold yourself accountable for implementing your attention management strategy, and what steps can you take to maintain a growth mindset throughout the process?

7.3 TRACKING PROGRESS AND ADJUSTING YOUR APPROACH

As you implement your personalized attention management strategy, tracking your progress and making adjustments as needed is crucial. This section will guide monitoring your progress and fine-tuning your approach to achieve your attention management goals.

TRACKING PROGRESS

1. **Regular check-ins**: Schedule regular check-ins with yourself to assess your progress toward your attention management goals. These check-ins can be daily, weekly, or monthly, depending on your preferences and the nature of your goals.
2. **Document your journey**: Keep a journal, spreadsheet, or digital tool to record your progress, successes, and challenges. This documentation will help you reflect on your journey and provide valuable insights into your attention management improvement.
3. **Quantify your progress**: Use quantifiable metrics to measure your progress. For example, track the number of tasks you complete within a set timeframe, or measure the time you spend in a flow state.

ADJUSTING YOUR APPROACH

1. **Identify what's working and what's not**: Analyze your progress and determine which strategies are effective and which may need adjustments or replacement.
2. **Be flexible and adaptable**: Recognize that your initial action plan may need to change as you learn more about your attention management strengths and weaknesses. Be open to modifying your goals and strategies as needed.

3. **Seek feedback**: Share your progress with trusted colleagues, mentors, or friends who can provide constructive feedback and suggestions for improvement.

∿

KEY TAKEAWAYS

- Tracking progress and adjusting your approach is essential to an effective attention management strategy.
- Regular check-ins, documentation, and quantifiable metrics can help you monitor your progress and identify areas for improvement.
- Being flexible, adaptable, and open to feedback will enable you to fine-tune your attention management strategy and achieve your goals.

∿

REFLECTION QUESTIONS

1. How can you incorporate regular check-ins, documentation, and quantifiable metrics into your attention management improvement process?
2. How can you remain open and flexible to adjust your goals and strategies as you progress in your attention management journey?
3. How can you leverage feedback from trusted colleagues, mentors, or friends to improve your attention management strategy and enhance productivity?

7.4 PRACTICAL EXAMPLE: A SUCCESSFUL TECHNICAL PROFESSIONAL'S ATTENTION MANAGEMENT JOURNEY

In this sub-chapter, we will explore the attention management journey of Sarah, a successful software developer, to illustrate how implementing an effective attention management strategy can lead to improved productivity, creativity, and job satisfaction.

SARAH'S CHALLENGES

Sarah struggled with managing her attention while juggling multiple projects, meetings, and deadlines. She frequently felt overwhelmed, leading to decreased focus and a decline in her work quality.

ASSESSING AND CREATING AN ACTION PLAN

Sarah began by assessing her current attention management skills and identifying areas for improvement. She realized she needed to prioritize, control distractions, and maximize her attention.

Sarah's action plan included the following goals:

1. Use the Eisenhower Matrix to prioritize her tasks.
2. Implement the Pomodoro Technique to improve focus and mindfulness.
3. Create a distraction-free workspace to minimize interruptions.

IMPLEMENTING AND TRACKING PROGRESS

Sarah committed to her action plan, sharing her goals with a colleague to ensure accountability. She tracked her progress using a spreadsheet, monitoring the number of completed tasks and time spent in focused work sessions.

ADJUSTING THE APPROACH

Over time, Sarah noticed improvements in her attention management. However, the Pomodoro Technique's rigid intervals didn't suit her work style. She adjusted her approach, experimenting with different time intervals and incorporating regular breaks to maintain focus.

POSITIVE OUTCOMES

As a result of her attention management journey, Sarah experienced increased productivity, better work quality, and a greater sense of control over her tasks. She also discovered that her improved focus led to more innovative and creative solutions in her work.

~

KEY TAKEAWAYS

- Assessing attention management skills, creating an action plan, and tracking progress are crucial steps in an effective attention management journey.
- Being open to adjusting strategies and goals and seeking feedback can lead to a more successful outcome.
- Attention management improvement can increase productivity, creativity, and overall job satisfaction.

~

REFLECTION QUESTIONS

1. What aspects of Sarah's attention management journey resonate with your experiences or challenges?
2. How can you apply Sarah's journey's lessons to your attention management strategy and goals?

3. What potential positive outcomes might you experience from implementing an effective attention management strategy in your professional life?

CONCLUSION

THE LIFELONG PURSUIT OF ATTENTION MANAGEMENT MASTERY

As you progress through your attention management journey, it's important to recognize that mastery is an ongoing pursuit. Continual improvement, adaptation, and growth are essential in maintaining high focus and productivity throughout your professional life.

EMBRACING THE JOURNEY

1. **Acknowledge progress**: Celebrate your achievements and recognize your progress in your attention management journey. Use these successes as motivation to keep improving.
2. **Stay curious**: Continue exploring new techniques, strategies, and tools to help you manage your attention more effectively. Stay open to learning and trying new approaches.
3. **Cultivate resilience**: Understand that setbacks and obstacles are part of the journey. Develop the resilience to learn from these challenges and use them to fuel your growth.

4. **Reassess and refine**: Regularly reassess your attention management skills and adjust your strategies and goals. This continuous refinement will help you stay on track and maintain momentum.

THE IMPACT OF ATTENTION MANAGEMENT MASTERY

As you work towards mastering attention management, you'll likely notice positive changes in multiple areas of your professional and personal life. These can include:

- Improved productivity and efficiency.
- Increased creativity and innovation.
- Enhanced decision-making abilities.
- Greater work-life balance.
- A more fulfilling and meaningful professional experience.

~

KEY TAKEAWAYS

- Attention management mastery is a lifelong pursuit that requires continuous improvement, adaptation, and growth.
- Embrace the journey by acknowledging progress, staying curious, cultivating resilience, and reassessing and refining your strategies and goals.
- Mastery of attention management can lead to numerous positive outcomes in your professional and personal life.

~

REFLECTION QUESTIONS

1. How can you maintain motivation and momentum in your attention management journey, despite encountering challenges and setbacks?
2. What strategies or habits can you develop to ensure continuous improvement and growth in attention management skills?
3. How do you envision the impact of attention management mastery on your professional and personal life?

CONTINUING YOUR ATTENTION MANAGEMENT JOURNEY

As you continue your attention management journey, it's essential to maintain focus on your goals, stay open to new strategies, and embrace the ongoing process of growth and development. Here are some suggestions for moving forward:

STAY COMMITTED

1. **Set long-term goals**: Establish long-term attention management goals that align with your personal and professional aspirations. These goals will help guide your progress and maintain your motivation.
2. **Track your progress**: Use a tracking system to monitor your progress, evaluate your strategies' effectiveness, and identify improvement areas.
3. **Seek support**: Engage with a community of like-minded individuals, mentors, or coaches who can offer guidance, encouragement, and accountability throughout your journey.

STAY INFORMED

1. **Keep learning**: Stay informed about new research, techniques, and tools related to attention management. Be open to incorporating new strategies into your practice.
2. **Attend workshops and conferences**: Participate in workshops, seminars, or webinars focusing on attention management to deepen your understanding and expand your network.
3. **Share your knowledge**: Share your experiences and knowledge with others within your professional circle and beyond. This helps others and reinforces your understanding of attention management principles.

∼

KEY TAKEAWAYS

- Continuing your attention management journey requires commitment, ongoing learning, and the willingness to adapt to new strategies and techniques.
- Stay committed by setting long-term goals, tracking progress, and seeking support from mentors or a community.
- Stay informed by continuing your education, attending workshops and conferences, and sharing your knowledge.

∼

REFLECTION QUESTIONS

1. How will you maintain your commitment to your attention management journey and stay focused on your long-term goals?
2. What steps will you take to stay informed about new research, techniques, and tools related to attention management?
3. How can you leverage your experiences and knowledge to help others in their attention management journey while reinforcing your understanding?

∼

BIBLIOGRAPHY

BOOKS AND ARTICLES

The following books and articles provide valuable insights and information on attention management, productivity, mindfulness, and related topics. These resources can serve as a foundation for further exploration and deepening your understanding of the concepts discussed in this book.

BOOKS

1. Newport, C. (2016). *Deep Work: Rules for Focused Success in a Distracted World*. Grand Central Publishing.
2. Morgenstern, J. (2004). *Time Management from the Inside Out: The Foolproof System for Taking Control of Your Schedule and Your Life*. Henry Holt and Company.
3. Duhigg, C. (2014). *The Power of Habit: Why We Do What We Do in Life and Business*. Random House.
4. Covey, S. R. (2013). *The 7 Habits of Highly Effective People: Powerful Lessons in Personal Change*. Simon & Schuster.
5. Goldsmith, M., & Reiter, M. (2015). *Triggers: Creating Behavior That Lasts-- Becoming the Person You Want to Be*. Crown Business.
6. Kabat-Zinn, J. (1994). *Wherever You Go, There You Are: Mindfulness Meditation in Everyday Life*. Hyperion.
7. Csikszentmihalyi, M. (2008). *Flow: The Psychology of Optimal Experience*. Harper Perennial Modern Classics.
8. Allen, D. (2015). *Getting Things Done: The Art of Stress-Free Productivity*. Penguin Books.

ARTICLES

1. Mark, G., Gudith, D., & Klocke, U. (2008). The Cost of Interrupted Work: More Speed and Stress. *Proceedings of the SIGCHI Conference on Human Factors in Computing Systems*, 107-110. DOI: 10.1145/1357054.1357072

2. Killingsworth, M. A., & Gilbert, D. T. (2010). A Wandering Mind is an Unhappy Mind. *Science*, 330(6006), 932. DOI: 10.1126/science.1192439

3. Iqbal, S. T., & Bailey, B. P. (2007). Investigating the Effectiveness of Mental Workload as a Predictor of Opportune Moments for Interruption. *Extended Abstracts on Human Factors in Computing Systems*, 1489-1492. DOI: 10.1145/1240866.1241020

4. Jett, Q. R., & George, J. M. (2003). Work Interrupted: A Closer Look at the Role of Interruptions in Organizational Life. *Academy of Management Review*, 28(3), 494-507. DOI: 10.5465/amr.2003.10196791

These books and articles can serve as a starting point for deepening your knowledge and understanding of attention management principles and techniques. As you continue your journey, explore additional resources, workshops, and conferences to stay up-to-date with the latest research and strategies.

RESEARCH STUDIES

The following research studies offer empirical evidence and insights into attention management, productivity, focus, and related topics. These studies can help you understand the scientific foundations of the concepts discussed in this book and serve as a basis for further exploration.

1. Kahneman, D., & Tversky, A. (1979). Prospect Theory: An Analysis of Decision under Risk. *Econometrica*, 47(2), 263-291. DOI: 10.2307/1914185

2. Baumeister, R. F., Bratslavsky, E., Muraven, M., & Tice, D. M. (1998). Ego Depletion: Is the Active Self a Limited Resource? *Journal of Personality and Social Psychology*, 74(5), 1252-1265. DOI: 10.1037/0022-3514.74.5.1252

3. Kirschner, P. A., Karpinski, A. C., Ozer, I., Mellott, J. A., & Ochwo, P. (2018). An Exploration of the Distracting Effects of Music on the Cognitive Test Performance of Introverts and Extraverts. *Applied Cognitive Psychology*, 32(4), 478-487. DOI: 10.1002/acp.3437

4. Marois, R., & Ivanoff, J. (2005). Capacity Limits of Information Processing in the Brain. *Trends in Cognitive Sciences*, 9(6), 296-305. DOI: 10.1016/j.tics.2005.04.010

5. Vohs, K. D., Redden, J. P., & Rahinel, R. (2013). Physical Order Produces Healthy Choices, Generosity, and Conventionality, Whereas Disorder Produces Creativity. *Psychological Science*, 24(9), 1860-1867. DOI: 10.1177/0956797613480186

6. Macan, T. H., Shahani, C., Dipboye, R. L., & Phillips, A. P. (1990). College Students' Time Management: Correlations with Academic Performance and

Stress. *Journal of Educational Psychology*, 82(4), 760-768. DOI: 10.1037/0022-0663.82.4.760

7. Tang, Y. Y., & Posner, M. I. (2009). Attention Training and Attention State Training. *Trends in Cognitive Sciences*, 13(5), 222-227. DOI: 10.1016/j.tics.2009.01.009

8. Goleman, D., & Davidson, R. J. (2017). The Science of Meditation. *Scientific American*, 317(3), 26-33. DOI: 10.1038/scientificamerican0917-26

These research studies provide a scientific foundation for understanding attention management, productivity, and related topics. As you continue your journey, keep an eye on the latest research to stay informed and up-to-date with new findings and best practices.

ONLINE RESOURCES

The following online resources offer valuable information, tools, and insights into attention management, productivity, focus, and related topics. These resources can help you stay updated on the latest techniques and strategies for effectively managing your attention.

WEBSITES AND BLOGS

1. Nir and Far: A blog by Nir Eyal, author of "Indistractable" and "Hooked," explores habit-forming products and the psychology of attention and focus.
2. Zen Habits: A blog by Leo Babauta that focuses on minimalism, mindfulness, and productivity.
3. Cal Newport's Study Hacks: A blog by Cal Newport, author of "Deep Work" and "Digital Minimalism," discusses focused work and living strategies.
4. RescueTime Blog: Articles and resources on productivity, time management, and digital wellness from the team behind the RescueTime time-tracking app.

APPS AND TOOLS

1. RescueTime. A time-tracking app that helps you understand how you spend your time on your devices and provides insights to improve your focus and productivity.

2. Todoist: A task management app that helps you organize and prioritize your tasks.

3. Focus@Will: A music service designed to help you concentrate and increase your productivity.

4. Headspace: A meditation app that offers guided mindfulness exercises to improve focus, reduce stress, and increase well-being.

ONLINE COURSES AND WORKSHOPS

1. Coursera - Learning How to Learn: A free online course that teaches effective learning and productivity techniques.

2. Udemy - Master Your Focus: A Practical Guide: A paid online course that provides strategies for improving focus and attention management.

3. LinkedIn Learning - Time Management Fundamentals: A paid online course that covers essential time management skills and strategies.

These online resources offer a wealth of information and practical tools to help you manage your attention effectively. As you continue your attention management journey, explore new resources and stay connected to experts and thought leaders to stay informed about the latest strategies and techniques.

∾

BONUS COMPANION GUIDE

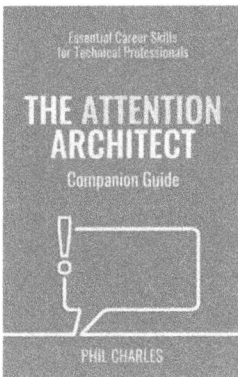

The Companion Guide complements *The Attention Architect* providing a fillable PDF with all the reflection questions from the book so you can work along and document your responses.

This book is only available to readers who have purchased the book!

Download your copy here:

https://bit.ly/attention-companionguide

ABOUT THE AUTHOR

Phil Charles is the author of a series of practical guides to help technical professionals build habits, develop focus, thinking, and analysis skills, and get things done with less stress. He focuses on critical skills and knowledge to improve productivity and get results.

As a technical professional with wide-ranging experience in government, consulting, and academia, Phil is particularly concerned about the challenges facing technical professionals and the limited opportunities to develop the essential non-technical career skills needed for professionals to be successful. Assessed as an INTJ, Phil is an analytical problem-solver seeking to improve systems and processes, seeking possibilities for improvement, whether at work or at home, hence his interest in essential non-technical career skills.

You can contact the author by email: phil@professionalpractice.academy

PROFESSIONAL PRACTICE ACADEMY

The Professional Practice Academy provides technical professionals with essential career skills and knowledge, focusing on non-technical skills like focus, decision-making, problem-solving, critical thinking, and managing time. Technical professionals need to lay a solid foundation to be successful – success is built on daily positive actions – and protect their future.

Professional Practice Academy https://professionalpractice.academy

A range of practical online courses to build your professional practice is available at ProSkills https://www.proskills.courses

~

OTHER BOOKS BY THE AUTHOR

See Phil Charles' author page: https://books2read.com/philcharles

Series: Essential Career Skills for Technical Professionals

Master Your Focus Today: *Learn How to Focus Better, Identify Your Distractions, and Organize Your Week*

Master the Habits of Effective People: Transformative Daily Practices for High Achievement to Align Your Professional Life.

~

www.ingramcontent.com/pod-product-compliance
Lightning Source LLC
Chambersburg PA
CBHW031604040426
42452CB00006B/402